The One Week Way
to Personal Success

The One Week Way
to Personal Success

John O'Keeffe

Thorsons
An Imprint of HarperCollins*Publishers*

Thorsons
An Imprint of HarperCollins*Publishers*
77–85 Fulham Palace Road,
Hammersmith, London W6 8JB

Published by Thorsons 1992
1   3   5   7   9   10   8   6   4   2

A catalogue record for this book
is available from the British Library

ISBN 0 7225 2599 0

Typeset by Harper Phototypesetters Limited,
Northampton, England
Printed in Great Britain by
HarperCollinsManufacturingGlasgow

Contents

This book is dedicated to Jeannie
who encouraged me to write it down
and to
Tim, Sam and Kelly
for whom it is written

Why this book?

It Gives You The Special O'Keeffe One Week Way to Success

If you had read the book *How to develop a Superpower Memory* you would have learnt a method of remembering the order of 52 playing cards in a randomly shuffled pack. It would only take you about 5 hours to learn how to do it. Before knowing the method, though, you would doubtless think it an impossible task, let alone one you could learn to do in just a few hours. But the method makes it easy – once you know how. Magic tricks are also easy – once you know how.

Similarly, if you had read the book *Faster Reading* you would have learnt to read ten times faster than you can now. Those who have only heard of faster reading, and not practised it, will be sceptical. But those who have learnt the special method will realize how very fast our minds can take in information through the eye; especially if we can find a way to avoid the tedious, slow, school-taught method of silently sounding out each word as we read. You are probably doing just that as you read this. The mind can actually take in written information at about 30 times the speed at which one can normally read. But you have to learn the method. The method makes it easy – once you know how.

The One Week Way to Personal Success also gives you a method. And because feeling successful and happy personally is so important to each of us, this is likely to be one of the most valuable books you will ever read. This method will, even if you only apply part of it, help you to make:

- next year the best year of your life
- next month the best month of your life
- next week the best week of your life
- tomorrow the best day of your life

It will take you no more than seven days to put the method fully into practice. From that moment on, you will truly believe that you can be successful, and you will feel more and more successful with every day.

The One Week Way Applies to You

It is not for someone else. It is not one of those methods you can read and 'pooh-pooh'. It is not something that is 'all very well, but it wouldn't work for me'.

It isn't written especially for businessmen, or housewives, or for young people, or for those going through their mid-life crisis. It isn't written just for office workers, or for those with a regular job.

This method applies to any and every individual. In fact it is precisely because we are all different that it works.

It works for you no matter who you are, what you do, or how old you are. It is something you will want to pass on to your friends and loved ones; to teach your children as they learn about life.

But, most of all, it will help you.

This Special Way is Valuable

Leading international companies can, over a period of time, pay in total approximately £10,000 per person to consultants and training specialists, to get the essence of such a system to their managers.

It can be yours for the price of one small book.

The One Week Way Works

This book is not written by a psychologist or by a management theorist. It is written by someone who actually uses this method to achieve personal success and who wants simply to pass it on.

Each of us will want to achieve different things. But the

system works for whatever you want to do. It has helped me to my own personal successes. In 1988, at the age of just 38 I became Managing Director of Procter & Gamble in the UK, a £1 billion company. You may not know the company, but if I tell you some of its products you'll know it's big – Pampers, Ariel, Daz, Fairy Liquid, Flash, Lenor, Camay.

I used the system to become an international hockey player for England at just l9, and also used it to retire from the sport at 2l.

I used it to learn Mandarin, even though I'm a complete non-linguist. I'm not a millionaire, but I have enough money.

I've used it to have some great times in my life: achieving a dream of working and living in Greece and staying on 26 Greek islands; enjoying 'second honeymoons' in Bali, Hong Kong, Bangkok, Phuket, Hawaii and the Philippines; spending a year in the US with my family seeing the sights, from New York to the Grand Canyon, from Texas to the West Coast; having the thrill of starting up businesses from scratch in Yemen and Oman, Dubai and Abu Dhabi, Bahrain and Qatar; having a house in Switzerland overlooking Lake Geneva, with views across to Mont Blanc, where the whole family learned to ski. I've used the system to play par golf for l4 holes (but haven't yet sustained it for l8 . . .). This way to personal success works.

The One Week Way is Simple

You Can Learn it in Seven days

There are just seven steps, each of which will be covered in detail:

Day 1 Consider What Success Means to You
Day 2 Aim High
Day 3 Work Out What You Want
Day 4 Manage Your Life-Time
Day 5 Manage Your Self
Day 6 Get Others to do What You Want
Day 7 Do Something Next

. . . And Easy to Use

You need just three things:

● this book
● a pocket diary
● a pocket notebook

Start reading this book on the train or bus and in any spare minutes you have. Next time you are in a newsagents, buy a small pocket notebook and a pocket diary if you don't already have them.

Within one week, you will be using your notebook and your spare time to work out exactly what you want, and what you can do to get it. You will be feeling great as you plan to make next year the best year of your life, next month the best month, next week the best week and tomorrow the best day.

But first, a quiz . . .

How well am I doing now?

Quickly go through the questions. For each statement, tick how true you think it is in your case, or whether it's untrue.

	Very True	Some what True	Mainly Untrue	Un-true	Very Untrue
1 I don't know exactly what success would be for me					
2 I don't know *exactly* what I would do if I had six months to live					
3 I don't know what I would do if I inherited a million pounds tomorrow					
4 I don't know what would make next year a successful year for me					
5 I don't know how to make next month the best of my life					
6 I don't know what would make tomorrow a great day for me					
7 I'm not sure I have the ability to be really successful					

	Very True	Some what True	Mainly Untrue	Un- true	Very Untrue
8 Others who are successful are generally luckier than me					
9 Others who are successful have had a better start than I've had – through education or money from their family					
10 Others who are successful are more clever than me					
11 I feel I'm not anything special					
12 Others who are successful generally have more 'connections' than I have					
13 I wish I didn't have to do half the things I'm doing					
14 It's too late to make a big change in my life now					
15 Much of what I do is because others expect it of me					
16 I feel I don't have the right balance of things in my life					
17 I wonder if I'd be better off doing something else . . .					
18 I wish I'd done something else for a job					
19 I wonder if my life couldn't be more exciting					
20 I wish I was living somewhere else					
21 I often feel bored or frustrated					

	Very True	Some what True	Mainly Untrue	Un- true	Very Untrue
22 Others seem to have a better life than I have					
23 I feel in a bit of a rut					
24 I think about how difficult my life is					
25 I don't know exactly what I want in the future					
26 I wish I was doing another job					
27 I often think Thank God it's Friday					
28 I find time just flies					
29 I really don't have outside interests					
30 I have too little time to do what I really want to do					
31 I put things off until later					
32 Routine things take up most of my time					
33 I feel I don't have time for myself					
34 I sometimes feel buried with everything I have to do					
35 I wish it was time to go home					
36 I start things and don't continue with them					
37 I feel tired at the end of the day and just want to watch TV					
38 I feel I can't afford what I want					
39 I get frustrated and annoyed at what others say					
40 I think about what others think of me					

	Very True	Some what True	Mainly Untrue	Un- true	Very Untrue
41 I think about 'what I could have said' in situations					
42 I often feel unappreciated					
43 I often have bad days					
44 Some days go from bad to worse					
45 I sometimes feel negative and depressed when I get up					
46 I remember bad things which happened yesterday or last week					
47 I often worry about things					
48 I feel people sometimes judge me unfairly					
49 I get concerned about everything I have to do, and what isn't done					
50 I think most people sometimes think negatively about me					
51 I don't like Monday mornings					
52 I could list, now, ten things that make me feel really rotten					
54 I often get tense or irritated					
55 I feel the world is against me					
56 I often criticize other people					
57 I put my views across, before I fully listen to those of other people					
58 I rarely tell people how good I think they are					

	Very True	Some what True	Mainly Untrue	Un- true	Very Untrue
59 I often contradict others					
60 I find myself arguing with people					
61 I don't like to bargain					
62 I am not able to say 'No' to requests of me					
63 I feel I don't do well in a negotiation					
64 I don't like to ask people for favours					
65 I feel I could get more fun out of life					

Now award yourself points for each of the 50 statements as follows:

Very True 1
Somewhat True 2
Mainly Untrue 3
Untrue 4
Very Untrue 5

Count up your total.

If your total is less than 200 out of a possible 325, you will get great benefit from the method in this book.

Between 200 and 250 you have a good sense of how to be successful, but the method will give you a helpful framework to turn that sense into actual achievement.

If your score is 250 – 300 you are probably already fairly successful but could still do with a refresher.

Above 300, you have unfortunately spent your money in vain. But you will know somebody to whom you could give this book, and who would get considerable benefit from it. So your investment is far from wasted.

Whatever your score – in the 100 – 300 bracket – let's now examine where you want to go from here . . .

Day 1

Consider What
Success Means to You

Many people say they want to be successful. Each and every recruit to our company says it. We wouldn't hire them if they didn't. But few have worked out exactly what 'success' means to them.

My method defines success as follows:

Success is to choose exactly what you want; then achieve it.

Both parts of this idea are equally important. There are many 'achievers' who end up not feeling fully successful because they didn't take time right at the start to choose what they really wanted. When they 'got there', they didn't feel really happy; and they are full of 'wish I'd also done this', or 'I regret that'. A symptom of this is the fact that a lot of so-called successful people have drink, drug, or marriage problems. They are not totally 'personally successful'.

Choosing the balance of what you want is just as important as achieving any single item.

At the same time, how often have you felt stuck in a rut, bored, fed up and listless, thinking life is dull? The problem is not knowing what you really want, so you have no chance of feeling good by reaching out to get it. The secret of feeling successful is to:

Regularly think about and choose what you want, and then achieve it.

Out of this comes a sense of personal worth; a sense of feeling good and fulfilled (instead of feeling frustrated and unfulfilled).

If you think in advance of what will make next year your best year, next month your best month, next week your best week, and tomorrow your best day – and then take steps to achieve these things – you will, indeed, feel successful and happy.

There are four principles to keep in mind as you work to realize what success is for you:

Principle 1

Your Choice of What You Want Should Cover the Broad Areas of Life

These include for example career, personal growth, personal relationships, material things, social activities, sport and leisure, friends, marriage, family, sex, hobbies and so on:

- I would like to own my own business
- I would like to have a baby
- I would like to be able to paint
- I would like to own a Porsche
- I would like to get on better with my parents
- I would like better sex
- I would like to know my children better

Many so-called successful people have not considered all the broad areas of life, and so end up not being personally successful. There are probably as many examples of people feeling unfulfilled and unsuccessful because they've chosen wrong, as there are examples of people feeling bad because they've failed to achieve what they chose. For example those who:

● do well in their careers but never see their children as they grow up, and regret it.
● sacrifice too much to become rich, have an unhappy personal life, and regret it.
● work hard and die young (and, however beloved of the Gods, never survive to find out where they went wrong . . .).
● work to get money to pass on to their children, only to find their children would have preferred to have more of their time than their money.

This is not to say that everyone must have balanced goals across the various life areas. Many individuals will want to be single-minded in just one area, if necessary to the exclusion of others. The key to personal success is to have chosen to aim for, rather than drift into, a particular balance. If you positively make a choice, and then achieve it, you'll feel successful.

Principle 2

It's What You Want That's Important to Your Success, Not What Others Want For You

Learn what it is you want. Not what your parents or family or friends want you to want – unless of course you want to please them that way (or it happens to coincide with your own aims for yourself). Not what people you know have wanted or done. Not what you think you ought to want; or what you think you ought to do, but what you really want. The world is full of 'might-have-beens' and 'wish-I-hads':

- I drifted into it because my parents did it, but I wish I had been something different.
- It was sort of expected of me, and I can't really remember actually deciding to do it. Now it's too late. I wish I had . . .
- At the time everyone was doing it. But looking back, I wish I had . . .

Learn the principle that true success will come only from understanding what you yourself want, not what others want for you.

Principle 3

What You Want Changes With Time

What you want can and should be different this year from what it was five years ago, and from what you'll want in five years' time. So it should, as you develop as a person, and the environment in which you are developing changes too. What you want at 20 is not the same as what you will want at 30. What you want when there's a war on is not the same as what you want when there is peace. Good planning and adaptability can go a long way to countering the old adage: 'If youth knew; if age could'.

So, periodically, you can and should revise your choice of goals, to accommodate the next stage of your life.

Principle 4

What You Want Needs To Have a Timescale

Becoming a millionaire in two years' time is not the same thing as making it in 30 years. They involve different trade-offs:

- doing it in two years requires very hard work, high risk-taking, or luck. For example, you could sell your house, put the money on a bet on a horse, and possibly succeed. Or save for two years and put the total on a high risk investment, and succeed. However the implications on the rest of your lifestyle if you fail, are very big.

- on the other hand, becoming a millionaire in 30 years may be possible if you inherit a house without a mortgage and just let its value gently appreciate over 30 years at ten per cent a year.

By putting a time-scale on what you want, it helps you identify the trade-offs that may be needed, and what is the exact balance that will represent success for you as an individual.

If you adopt these four principles you can start to realize what success is, for you. Day 3, 'Work Out What You Want', will help you further. Once you are choosing what you want, and then achieving it, you will feel successful. It is a personal sense of worth. A sense of achievement. A sense of feeling good and fulfilled versus feeling frustrated and unfulfilled.

But before we go any further, let's see how realistic it is for you to think you can achieve what you want . . .

Day 2

Aim High

You may say that it's all very well thinking about what you want, but there is no chance of getting it. It just isn't realistic, so it's a waste of time going through the exercise.

This just isn't true. Don't believe that those people who are successful in their lives are necessarily smarter, harder-working, luckier, better educated, or even come from richer families than you. Don't think you have less chance of being successful than others. In fact you have more chance – just by seeking to learn a method to be successful, as you are now doing.

Everyone who follows this method will be successful. The only differences will arise from how often and how diligently you apply it.

No matter what your background, abilities or achievements so far, there are three realizations you can now make which will allow you to aim higher in what you want for yourself.

Realization 1

I Have Unique Abilities That Are Far More Valuable Than I Think

You are unique. Never in the history of man has there been anyone exactly like you, nor will there be again. This is absolutely true.

No one else in the world has exactly the same mind as you, looks at things exactly the way you do, has the same gut feelings that you do, imagines things the way you do, acts the way you do.

You are you because you inherited a unique mix of chromosomes from your father and mother, comprising in total thousands of genes. Just one gene can change the make-up of a person. Thus, even if your parents had thousands of children, they would not produce someone exactly like you. Just consider for a moment how different you are from your own brothers and sisters.

If you don't feel unique, just travel the world and try to find someone who even looks exactly like you. You will not find anyone, let alone someone who also acts like you, thinks like you, or can do things the way you can.

If you don't feel unique, just consider your fingerprints. If just the patterns on a piece of skin can be truly unique, then the whole person surely is.

There is no-one else in the world who has the same accumulation of knowledge you have; the same collection of abilities or experiences; the same way of looking at things; the same personality and power . . .

It is your unique abilities that will, in the end, help you to achieve your personal balance of what you want. You are different from anyone else, and you should feel good about it because, in the end, you will feel successful in a way that no-one else can exactly match.

Realization 2

It Isn't My IQ That Matters, Or My Education, But How Well I Learn to Use My Thinking Power Practically

The thinking that guides your intelligence is much more important than how much intelligence you have. How many people do you know who are supposedly intelligent but seem to think and act in a way that isn't at all practical; in a way that won't really help them succeed?

Our brains are definitely underused, no matter what our IQ. There is 100 times more potential in learning better to use the thinking power we have, than in having a different or higher IQ.

You don't need a bigger brain to succeed. You just need to really drive and apply the brain you have. The brain is a fantastic biological computer. It has been calculated that all the electrical and electronic connections of the world's telephone systems, if put together in the same way as a brain, would be only as big as a raisin. Your own brain is far bigger and more powerful.

No-one – not you or I, nor anyone who has ever lived – has got close to using the full power of his or her brain, mind, or self.

This book will, however, help you to use more of your brain power in practical ways that can help you succeed:

- positive thinking instead of negative
- big thinking instead of small
- forward thinking instead of backward looking
- lateral thinking instead of tunnel vision
- believing you can succeed instead of giving up or, worse still, never trying

You are learning all these now. They will give you greater advantages in succeeding than any difference in education or IQ.

Realization 3

I Can Learn How To Choose My Attitude And This, More Than Anything Else, Will Help Me To Succeed

You can't control where you were born, or how much money you had to start with, or how high your IQ is, or what others do to you or think of you.

But you can control what you do with what you were given, how you react to what happens to you and how you react to what others say about you.

We often blame other things: 'I'm too old/too young'; 'I didn't have enough money to start with'; 'I'm not intelligent enough'; 'I didn't get a proper education'; 'I've tried that before and it didn't work'; 'It's because of other people that I can't do it'.

But what really holds us back is our attitude: a negative way of looking on life; feeling fed up or sorry for ourselves; worrying; procrastinating; being lazy and wasting time.

But your attitude is your personal choice. You can learn to shape and control it. And by shaping your attitude you can make the most of what you have.

You can alter your life by altering your state of mind – most people are about as happy as they make up their minds to be . . .

A negative attitude is completely your own fault, no-one else's. Changing to a positive attitude can be the most important advantage you can give yourself to help you succeed.

No matter what your background, abilities and achievements these three realizations, or 'self-boosters', should help you aim high in what you want for yourself.

So remember:

● You have *unique abilities* that are a lot more valuable than you think.
● It isn't your IQ that matters, or your education, but *how well you learn to use your thinking power*, practically.
● You can learn to *choose and control your attitude* and this, more than anything, will help you succeed.

You *can* aim high, very high.

Let's now review on Day 3 how to decide exactly what you want to aim for . . .

Day 3

Work Out
What You Want

What Do You Want?

Most people spend more time thinking about their summer holidays than about their lives. By failing to plan you are actually planning to fail, because if you don't run your life, other people and events will run it for you.

Many people just go through the motions of living. They live and die without ever taking the time to think about their purpose in life and what they want out of it. Because they do not know exactly what they want out of life they can never get it, and never feel they've been successful. Because they don't know exactly where they are going, they never feel they are getting anywhere. They never enjoy the thrill that comes from being successful through choosing a goal and achieving it.

What goals do you want to choose?

Here are seven separate exercises to help you decide. Do them. Now. Use a pen and paper, or jot down your answers in pencil in this book (you can always rub them out if you don't want others to see). Start now. Do them. These are key exercises to help you form your goals.

Exercise 1

My Life-Picture

Do this exercise in your pocket notebook.

The idea of this exercise is to get a picture of your life on one sheet of paper so that you can review it easily. Write 'Me' in the middle of a blank sheet of paper and put a circle round it. Next, think of all the roles you play – career person, spouse, parent, partner, sports player, writer, amateur actor, lover, housewife, cook, sister, and so on. Write each role on a line or spoke coming out from the central circle. Make a little circle at the end of each line. Now branch out from the little circle by putting in the people or things associated with that role, and the activities involved. Just keep on branching. Put things down as you think of them.

By the time you've finished, the whole page will be a picture full of the activities of your life. The picture will be as unique as your fingerprints. It is you.

You will see on page 32 the start of one Life-Picture. At this stage all the roles have been put in, and there has been a start on branching out the role of 'father' and 'lover' into the people or activities of that role. The picture should be built up to fill the whole page.

Page 33 shows another example of what the start of a Life-Picture might look like: all the roles are in, and a start is being made to branch out the role of 'ex-Teacher'.

Now do yours. Please start now. The secret is to get it all down, roughly. It doesn't matter about mistakes.

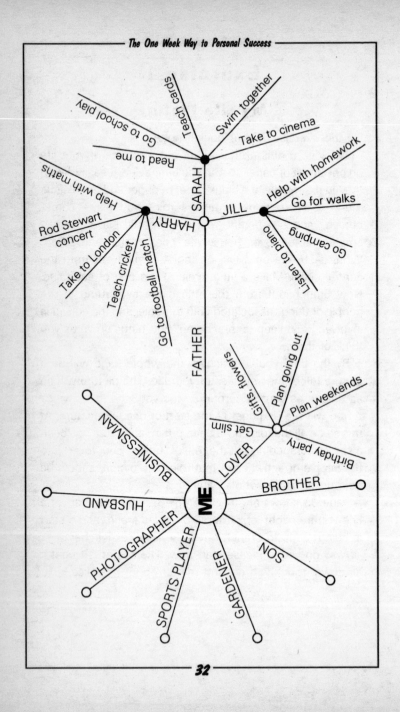

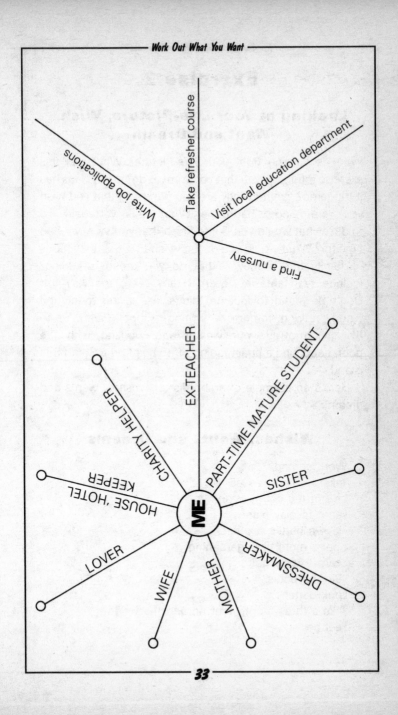

Exercise 2

Looking at Your Life-Picture, Wish, Want and Dream

What is missing from your Life-Picture? What has this exercise reminded you that you want to do? What ideas has it triggered? What exactly are you not doing that you wish you were doing or had done? What would you really like to do? What would you like to finish that you've never had time for? What would you do if it wasn't for the restrictions of family and money? What do you dream of doing? Include real fantasies, even if they seem too way-out. Don't be afraid to include things like sailing round the world, retiring tomorrow, writing a book, learning to fly, giving away your wealth and working with the poor, becoming a priest, going off to paint on a South Sea island . . .

Here's an example of a shortlist of 'wishes, wants and dreams':

Wishes, Wants and Dreams

Work abroad
Take evening classes
Live in the countryside
Learn to play piano
Have a better sex life
Spend more time gardening
Learn to play golf
Win the pools
Look better
Take a three-month tour around the world
Feel better

Build a house extension
Spend more time with the kids each day
Buy a dishwasher
Write more letters to friends

Write your wishes, wants and dreams list, now.

Exercise 3

Goals by Goal Area

List the areas in which you feel you may want to set and achieve goals, e.g. (a) work, (b) leisure and hobbies, (c) social activities, (d) material things, (e) personal life, (f) inter-personal relationships, and so on. Under each area draw up a list of goals. Here are some examples to get you started:

Work Goals

Become General Manager by age 40
Be the best salesman this month
Get a job abroad in the sun for three years
Find a way to work part-time
Get away from work on time three times a week
Start my own business
Become a monk
Become a politician

Inter-personal Relationship Goals

Ditch your current partner
Fall in love again with your current partner
Get to know your kids better
Meet your work colleagues socially
Get to know the neighbours
Make three new friends in the next month
Do one activity with each child alone each week
Have one evening out alone with your spouse each week

Leisure and Hobby Goals

Visit China
Learn to play a keyboard
See *Miss Saigon*
Do a parachute jump
Write a book

Social Goals

Join a club
Throw a dinner party each week
Get on the club committee
Take the lead in the next drama group production

Study Goals

Get a degree
Learn French
Start an evening pottery class
Read a book on memory improvement
Get a university entrance by correspondence course
Learn to work a computer
Learn to type
Join the Open University

Material Goals

Buy a fun sports car
Buy a dishwasher
Buy a comfortable new chair
Buy a bed you like
Earn enough money to retire
Buy a motorbike
Buy a weekend cottage
Move to a bigger house
Buy a present for yourself each month

Personal Goals

Read a 'how-to' book each month
Learn to be a better listener
Learn how to compliment others
Be a better lover
Stop smoking
Look smarter, sexier
Get contact lenses
Learn to forgive
Join the French Foreign Legion

Sports Goals

Take tennis lessons
Get a golf handicap under 20
Jog every day
Go to Wimbledon
Learn to scuba-dive
Join an exercise class

Now do your own list in your pocket notebook.

Exercise 4

Choose a Goal

Here is a list of 100 goals. Go through them and tick those that are closest to the goals *you* want. (Single tick those that are similar to what you want, but need to be adapted. Double tick those that are exactly what you need). Then make your own list in your notebook.

Have a better relationship with my children
Have more time for my hobbies
Learn to say sorry sincerely when I'm at fault
Take three holidays a year
Earn more money
Flirt more effectively
Buy nicer clothes
Move to a bigger house
Play a musical instrument
Carry on interesting dinner party conversation
Make a tour of Europe
Feel in less of a rut
Not feel under pressure at work
Get a job I enjoy more
Find it easier to ask someone out
Go on a safari
Deal better with boring people
Hold more dinner parties
Stand up for myself better
Be more adventurous in bed
Lose weight
Drop out
Get a pet

Have better holidays
Get on the squash team
Do charity work
Get on better with my brothers/sisters
Get a new car
Get more time for myself
Live in the country
Lose weight
Have a better sex life
Be more active
Not feel I've wasted time
Be better at sport
Say how I really feel with my partner
Live in the sun
Be a better host/hostess
Be better at making business presentations
Not bring work home
Learn to say no
Be fitter
Get promoted at work
Have more spare time interests
Get on better with my parents
Get others to cooperate in the house/at work
Come across better in meetings
Get more time to play golf
Tell jokes
Not feel bored
Use my travel/commuting time better
Talk to people I don't know
Have more friends at work
Spend less time on homework
Find a new hobby
Ask for what I want

Learn to dance
Do better in exams
Get more balance in my life
Have less to do at work
Have a country cottage
Buy a yacht
Get into local politics
Handle criticism better
Drink less alcohol
Feel more confident
Have more shared interests with my partner
Start my own restaurant
Eat more varied meals
Get a dishwasher/video/new stereo
Get my boss's job
Get a new girlfriend/boyfriend
Get transferred to head office
Get new furniture
See more films or plays
Be appreciated more at work
Sleep in once a week
Earn money in my spare time
Learn to fly
Get rid of spots/stop biting nails/picking nose
Pass an exam
Visit a sex shop
Feel 'down' less often
Make a career change
Go out more
Decorate the house
Be better at meeting new people
Write a book
Have more energy

Buy a fun motorbike
Get a job which doesn't involve commuting
Be better at do-it-yourself
Listen to music more
Express myself better
Handle it better when others are unfair to me
Cook more adventurously
Learn to fly-fish

Exercise 5

Pick-Me-Ups and Put-Me-Downs

The idea of this exercise is to list your personal 'pick-me-ups' and 'put-me-downs'. Take any period, for instance last week or last month.

List all the things you remember distinctly liking: things that gave you a buzz or a sense of well-being; things you felt good about at the time. (These can be quite small events: a cup of real coffee first thing in the morning, a five-minute break to smell the roses, a new tie. Or they can be 'big' events like a promotion, a concert, dinner with an old schoolfriend . . .)

List separately all the things you remember specifically not liking; things that seemed to make you depressed or feel down; things that got you upset. (Again these can be small or big: no answer to a letter you wrote, a recommendation not accepted, an unexpected bill, the illness of a relative . . .)

A start to the lists could be:

Pick-me-ups

Going for a walk with the kids
A good film
Enjoying a book
Buying myself a new tie
Unexpected call from an old friend

Put-me-downs

Row with my partner
Feeling hung over after night out
Feeling fat and unfit
Office politics
Doing nothing at the weekend
Watching too much TV
Being unfairly criticized at work

Make your list here. Now.

It's a good idea to draw up lists like this every week, or as things actually happen that lift or depress you.

By looking at your list of pick-me-ups you will be able to identify which things you want more of in your life: the things that can help make today a good day and tomorrow even better.

Looking at the list of put-me-downs will enable you to identify what you could do to control, minimize and eliminate them from your life.

Try it with the lists you've just written:

Exercise 6

Lightning Will Strike Me

Assume you know that you are going to be struck by lightning six months from now. Write down how you would spend these last six months (anything is allowed here . . .):

Again, write a fuller account in your pocket notebook.

Exercise 7

My Funeral Oration

Write down what you would like to be said about you in the funeral oration at the end of your life. (Feel free to dream a little, include things you haven't yet done and perhaps might never do, but would love to do and be remembered for). Include comments on your character, or skills that perhaps you haven't yet achieved, but aspire to. Jot down here, now, what you'd like to have written on the gravestone or in the oration that would do full justice to your life when you're finally gone:

When you have a spare moment, write a fuller account in your pocket notebook.

Exercise 8

Next Steps

Now write in your pocket notebook the list of techniques available to help you think about choosing goals:

1 Life-picture
2 Wish, want and dream
3 Goals by goal area
4 Choose a goal
5 Pick-me-ups and put-me-downs
6 Lightning will strike me
7 My funeral oration

Use your pocket notebook to repeat and expand these exercises.

Looking at everything you've written in exercises 1-7, use your pocket notebook to record the answers to these questions:

1 If asked today what my lifetime goals are, they would be:
2 In a diary, in three years' time, I would like to be able to write that I had set out these goals and had achieved them:
3 Pick a date six months from now. Write down what you would like to have achieved by then:
4 Write down the things you can do to make tomorrow a better day:

Day 3 will have given you a good idea of what you want. Days 4 – 6 will help you work on how to get it. So let's look next at how to manage your time and not waste it . . .

Day 4

Manage Your
Life-Time

We all have many wishes, wants and dreams. The secret of success is to take the actions that will achieve them.

Time – quite literally your life-time – is your most valuable asset. If you have decided you want something, you must be prepared to donate some of your time towards achieving it, rather than spending, or even wasting, your time on other things. This process of time-allocation includes questioning all the things you currently spend your time on, including those you think you have no choice but to do. You will soon realize that there is *always* a choice: whether to go shopping once a fortnight instead of once a week; whether to attend a meeting; whether to watch TV for the next hour; resolving, for once, not to spend time cooking a meal, but have a snack and to spend the time saved on your pet project.

Many people think money is their most valuable asset. But if you waste money you will still have an opportunity to get some more. If you waste time, though, it's gone forever. You will have wasted a part of your life.

Most of us are careful with our money. We wouldn't throw away half our money or spend it on something absolutely useless. But most of us frequently throw away half our time, and parts of our life, on activities which can be almost totally useless to us or anyone else.

As Diamond Lil used to say: 'It's not the men in my life that matter; it's the life in my men'. It's the same with the years in your life, and the life in your years. Act and behave each day in the knowledge that life is a short but wonderful experience, and aim to make the very best of it.

There are just five lessons on how to manage your life-time. You've probably heard them all before, but don't really act on them. This chapter will make it easy for you to do just that.

Five Lessons on How to Manage Your Life-Time

1 Decide your priorities, and work at the most important first.
2 Do something to achieve your goals, and keep on doing it.
3 Make time for the things you want to do.
4 Don't do other things.
5 Keep up the momentum.

Lesson 1

Decide Your Priorities. Play in Your First Division

It's your choice, and choosing correctly is the first half of being successful? Which goals, once you've achieved them, will make you feel successful. Which goals, when you're working towards them, will help you feel good?

Decide which of your goals have the highest priority for you, and which the lower priority. Only you can decide. Identify the ones most important to you as being in your own First Division, the least important as your Third Division, and ones in the middle as Second Division. Concentrate on the ones in your First Division. This is where you want to play life.

What you need to do is to find a way to focus your time and life energy on those which you've already decided are important to you – and away from things you're doing which, when you think about it, aren't as important to you (we'll see how to go about this in Lesson 2). Don't play your life in the Third Division.

Return now to the list of goals in your notebook. Put them in order of First Division, Second Division, Third Division. Concentrate on the First Division.

For example you may decide:

First Division
Spend more time with the children
Work abroad
Learn golf
Second Division
Get a job abroad

Stop smoking
Tour Europe
Third Division
Do charity work
Write a book
Buy a new stereo

Think even more about the priorities within these goals. Remember, your top priority items will be the ones you will want to spend most of your time and effort on. You don't want to end up not trying hard, using the excuse, 'Well, I didn't really want to do that anyway'. So concentrate now on comparing your goals and working out which are the ones that are most important to you. A good exercise is to number each goal in order of importance.

Taking the example above, you may decide on the following order, with the following specific aims and time boundaries.

Top Priority (First Division)

1 Spend more time with the children – at least 1 hour with each individually and 2 hours on a joint activity each week.
2 Learn golf – to a handicap of 20, in 6 months.
3 Get a job abroad – this year.

You have now decided your priorities and where you want to put your time and effort.

Lesson 2

Work Towards Your Goal. Kick the Ball

As soon as you've decided on a First Division goal, work out exactly how to achieve it. There are two steps:

1 List quickly all the possible actions you can think of that might help
For example, in the goals above, you may list:
Learn Golf, to a 20 handicap, in 6 months

find out if any friend has a teaching video they might lend you.
borrow teaching books from the library.
make a list of each person you know who plays golf and ask them what they think is the best way to learn.
list local driving ranges from the Yellow Pages.
ring up each one and ask if they do lessons for beginners, their prices, etc.
ask them if you can borrow a few clubs to learn with.
make a list of when you could spare 1 hour or half an hour, two or three times a week, e.g. before breakfast; on the way back from work; lunch hour if it's close enough; late at night in the summer.

You can probably think of several other actions you might take.

2 Select from the possible actions list those which would most help you achieve your goal
Mark them 'A' if they would be a big help, 'B' if medium, 'C' if small. Focus on the 'A' activities. You'll then make

more progress by spending a short amount of time doing a little bit of an 'A' activity, than by doing a whole 'C'. Learn to break down the 'A' activities into little pieces and do a piece at a time.

In the example above you can decide for yourself which action on the list is likely to be the most helpful for you. If you are no good at learning from books, then that action would be a 'C'; if you don't know many golfers, asking their advice might be a 'C'. But for almost everyone, ringing around the local golf ranges will be an 'A'. Do a bit of work by starting to list your golfing friends or writing down all the golf range telephone numbers on a sheet of paper so that you can ring without needing the Yellow Pages. Do it *now*!

Pareto's Law

Remember – you don't have to do everything on any list of actions in order to achieve success. Pareto's Law states that 80% of results come from about 20% of any list of possible actions. If there is a list of ten things to do to help you towards a goal, two will probably get you most of the way. All you need to do is to find which they are. The 80/20 rule does work. Consider, for example, these truths:

- 80% of your time in the house is spent in 20% of the rooms.
- 80% of washing comes from the 20% of the wardrobe that's well used.
- 80% of sales come from 20% of customers.
- 80% of dirt is on the 20% of floor area that is highly used.
- 80% of sales come from 20% of the product line.

● 80% of phone call time is to 20% of your acquaintances.

Find the 20% that will get you most of the way to your goal, and work on it. Doing a little bit of the 20% is better than doing anything in the 80% sector.

Lesson 3

Make Time For the Things You Want to do

It is all very well having new goals, and lists of things to do, but how on earth can you fit them into a life where you already feel you don't have enough time?

There are four 'Working Models' to help you do this.

Live on the Top Floor of Life

Do What is Important rather than What is Urgent.

Think about all the activities you currently spend your time on. Ask yourself: 'How urgent are they?' 'How important are they?' 'What do I really want?'

Something that is urgent is not the same thing as something that is important. We all spend too much of our time on apparently urgent things (rushing to get somewhere by a certain time, answering this phone ringing now, going to the shops this morning, answering this letter now) that turn out not to be very important. Often the really important things don't get done because they are seldom urgent (having a better relationship with your children, making a will, changing an investment portfolio).

You need to focus your time on things that are important to you, both urgent and non-urgent, rather than have your life dictated by the things that are only urgent, whether they are important to you or not. The important things to you are those you have identified in your priority list as First Division projects.

In this working model of importance versus urgency, learn to classify your life according to what 'floor' you're living on. There are 4 basic floors – the Basement, Ground Floor, First Floor and Top Floor. You should aim to spend less and less of your time in the Basement of Life, and more and more on the Top Floor of Life.

The Floors of Life are as follows.

Basement

Your time is spent on things which are neither important nor urgent

Such things include:

Most newspaper reading

80% of TV watching

What else could you write down here?

Ground Floor

Your time is spent on things which, though urgent, are unimportant

Such things include:

Most interruptions

Most telephone calls

Dealing with the mail

Most things in today's timetable

What else could you write down here?

First Floor

Your time is spent on things which are both important and urgent

This includes most crises:

A loved one gets taken ill

Your car breaks down and needs fixing

What other ones could you include here?

Top Floor

Your time is spent on things which are important but not urgent

This includes things like:

Working out what you want in life

Having medical check-ups

Taking a step towards one of your goals

What other ones could you include here?

The more of your time you can spend working on the 'top floor' of life the more successful you will be. Working on the top floor will help prevent some of the important things from becoming urgent by becoming a crisis. How do you get to the top floor? Simple, take a mental lift, press the top button and go up. It's your choice. Measure each day by 'how much of it I spent on the top floor'. The more time you spend up there, the easier you'll find it to go up there again and even to stay up there.

Use Now-Time

Continually ask yourself, 'What's the best way to use these moments of my life, now? What's the best thing I can do with this 10 minutes, half hour, or hour of my life . . .which I'll never have again?'

The best way of using this time is often to do a little bit towards achieving a First Division goal.

Never use a few short minutes to do a 'C' activity to get it out of the way, or because there wasn't enough time to do an 'A' – that won't help you to win the First Division. You've already decided that a 'C' is less important, so why waste your life on it? By contrast, there is always some little thing you can do to help move towards your 'A', which is, after all, what is important to you.

In the golf example quoted earlier, the clear way to use now-time was to pick up the Yellow Pages and make a list of all golfing ranges where you might be able to take lessons. A second action would be to list the questions you'd ask each to get the necessary information.

Similarly, if you are working towards the goal of getting a job abroad, which seems a big task, what you can do NOW is list all the possible steps you can take. Once you've done that and put them in priority order, the best use of your time might be to send just one letter in the few minutes you have available to you, NOW.

Plan Your Week

This working model is particularly easy to use once you have listed and sorted the actions you need to take to achieve each of your top goals.

From these you can sit down with a pocket diary and work out 'what can I do this week to help me achieve my goals?' This is particularly good to do with other members of the family who might be involved – or who may be working at their own goals. Sunday is an ideal time to do this.

Sit down with your list of goals and actions and plan

which of them you could do, or start to do, during next week and when. Use your pocket diary to help.

A week is about the most effective period that any of us can use for planning. A day is too short to do a bit of all the things we want to do, and a month is too long – it leads to procrastination, and it can be difficult to plan so far ahead.

The purpose is not merely to plan to fill up time; the purpose is to think, at the beginning of the week, how, when and what you could do to help you to your goals. Write notes in your diary to remind you of which 'actions towards a goal' you're choosing to get done, and on which day.

Start Each Day With a 'To Do' List

Make a list, each morning, of everything you need to do on that particular day. This includes both personal items from your weekly planner, as well as work or home commitments. Don't bother with routine daily events that will happen anyway. Don't put down anything you know you won't get round to doing, just to make yourself feel busy and the day look full.

Put down high priority points which might not get done without special attention.

Now, *set priorities*. Mark your projects A, B or C:

- A are those things you *must do* today
- B are those things you *probably should do* today
- C are those things *it would be nice to do* today

Focus on your A's. Mark the most important one Al, the next A2 and so on.

Now, do first things first. Carry out your most important item, followed by the next most important, and so on.

There will often be important things to do that are difficult or unpleasant, and you may want to put them off. A good trick is to take one of these and do it early. Your sense of achievement will be high, you'll feel satisfied and already well on top of the day.

Lesson 4

Don't Do Other Things

There will often seem to be so many demands on your time that you can't get round to doing what is important to you. You will need to find ways to stop doing some of your current activities. Here are several ways to help:

Pursue effectiveness. Remember we are seeking effectiveness, which means doing the right things. This is different from efficiency, which is doing things right.

Be confident that doing only the right things means that you won't be doing other things. You don't aim to do everything.

Get an LBW Drawer (Let the Blighter Wait)

Dump into the drawer all the things you think are in category LBW – and just leave them there. Sometimes an LBW will become a B or even an A as a result of urgency. But not often. And when it does, deal with it as an 'A'. Periodically throw out the contents of the LBW drawer.

If you work in an office, much of your in-tray material can be put straight into your LBW drawer, or even better into a waste paper basket. At home, much of what comes through your letter box can go into an LBW drawer or a waste paper basket.

Don't feel guilty about the LBW drawer. Feel great! It frees you to focus on the things you've decided are important.

Operate a 'Won't Do' System

Don't:

1 do anything you can pass on to someone else to do
2 do anything just to please others because you fear their displeasure
3 do anything that is an unreasonable drain on your time
4 do anything others should be doing for themselves
5 do anything which, if you don't do it, is not that big a deal
6 do anything which, once you've done it, won't matter that much

If you decide, today, that these are your six new commandments and then follow them in home, office, school and club activities, you can release enormous chunks of time to do the things you really want to do – and should be doing.

Learn to Say 'No'.

Your time is *your* life, and you don't want to waste either. So it is acceptable to say 'No' because:

- that's not how you want to spend your time
- you choose not to do it
- you choose to do other things instead

The trick is to find a way to say 'No' that is acceptable to the person asking. There are some very simple things you can do to help your 'No' to be acceptable:

- refuse early, before people build an expectation that you may say yes
- be polite and pleasant
- give reasons why not
- offer an alternative suggestion on how the person might get help

Lesson 5

Keep Momentum

Sometimes it's just difficult to get going, or to keep going. Here are some various tips to help you keep momentum:

- Work out a list of little rewards for yourself, like buying yourself a small treat at lunch time, having another cup of coffee, taking a walk outside, reading the sports page of the newspaper. Make a 'little things for me' list in your notebook. Then, when faced with an unpleasant task, or a difficult one, promise yourself one of the 'little things' at the end of it. Make sure you really do reward yourself – you'll find it easier next time to start a difficult or unpleasant task.

- Get started now. If there's a difficult or unpleasant task, *do it first*. That really gets you rolling!
- Don't put things off. Do it now. NOW, NOW, NOW!
- Remember that you're in charge. It's your time. You're in control of it. Your choices make the difference. (And no-one else really cares).
- Check the decisions you're making. Are you really choosing? Or are you being driven by habit? Or by the demands of others? Or by escapism? Or by the spur of the moment? Or by default? Or are you really, consciously deciding how to use your time? Are you happy with the outcome? If not, change it!
- Identify your peak periods, when you are at your best. If you're good in the mornings, do 'A's then, not later when you're tired.
- Take time out to make more time. Use the weekly plan which you should be drawing up every Sunday. Each day, the first priority is to work out what are the most important things to do that day.
- Celebrate crossing out an 'A' once you've done it, or even a piece of an 'A'. Tell yourself how smart you are.

30 Ways I Manage my Life-Time

1   I love *not* doing 'C's, but just leaving them to sit there.
2   I don't worry at all about apparently 'being behind' on my paperwork – as long as I've dealt with the important bits.
3   I enjoy not answering letters (except from friends who I want to write to).
4   I enjoy leaving trivia to be handled when and if I feel like it.
5   I enjoy just leaving things in an LBW drawer.
6   I love identifying what's important to me and concentrating my time on that.
7   I don't waste time regretting failures.
8   I don't feel guilty about what I'm not doing.
9   If I wake up early, I get up early, even at 5a.m. This is the time when I'm 'at my best' and when there's no one else to interrupt me.
10 I don't bother working too late because I'm not much good when I'm tired.
11 I try to use railway station lounges and trains, which give me more high-quality time to think and plan, rather than airports and planes which give me poor-quality time because of their sense of hectic frustration.
12 I carry with me everywhere (a) a pocket notebook to work out and update my goals and my activities, (b) a pocket diary for weekly planning.
13 I use all my 'waiting time' – in any spare minutes I can work, on my own, towards my own success.

14 I review 'What we want to do towards our goals this week' with each member of the family every Sunday.

15 I set goals 'for a year' and find I revise them once every six months – the more successful I've been, the more often they need revising.

16 I plan a yearly timetable for holidays.

17 I plan weekends away – to get balance – and I do this several months ahead.

18 I do first things first.

19 I enjoy not answering the phone (and I try to avoid returning calls).

20 I never seek perfection (it's unattainable).

21 I have confidence in my judgement of priorities and stick to them in spite of difficulties.

22 I ask myself, would something terrible happen if I didn't do this, and if not, I don't do it.

23 I always use the 80/20 rule.

24 I never try to do everything I 'ought' to. (I never try to do everything).

25 I take time out to think.

26 I identify key projects for the next year, next six months, next month.

27 I keep pushing on what I think are the key projects.

28 I work to a 'To Do' list, with priorities.

29 I enjoy finding all the practical actions I can do now to further my goals; and feel great once I've taken a step.

30 I am continually asking myself, 'What's the best use of this moment, now?'

Next Steps

*1 Now write the following lessons in your pocket notebook
to remind you of tips to manage your life-time.*

Lesson 1

Decide my goals. Play in the First Division.

Lesson 2

Do something. Kick the ball.
  Do 'A' activities before 'B's or 'C's.
  Do a little part of an 'A' before a 'B' or a 'C'.

Lesson 3

Make time for the things I want to do.

    Live on the top floor of life. Work on important but not
    necessarily urgent things
    Use now-time
    Plan each week
    Start each day with a 'to do' list

Lesson 4

Don't do other things

    Pursue effectiveness, rather than efficiency
    Use an LBW drawer
    Operate a 'won't do' system
    Say No

Lesson 5

Keep up the momentum

2 Use your pocket notebook and pocket diary for weekly planning, and for 'to do' lists.

Now you know how to manage your life-time, let's move on to managing your Self.

Day 5

Manage Your Self

When reviewing the best way to manage your time, a key aspect is to 'keep up momentum'. The single biggest hindrance to getting things done, which stops your momentum, is you, yourself, indeed your 'self'.

We all have good days, and we all have bad days – good times and bad times, good moods and bad moods. To be successful, to achieve the things you want, you need to manage your 'Self' to make sure you have more good days and fewer bad ones.

Do you remember the day last week when you were hassled? Nothing went right. Trouble started early on, and it went from bad to worse. You got nothing done. But you went home absolutely exhausted, and ready for nothing but to slump in front of the TV.

The next day everything clicked into place. You got twenty times more done than you did the previous day. Yet you went home as fresh as a daisy, full of energy, and keen to go out.

The first day you were in a low – you got nothing done and you got tired. This was probably mostly caused by types of feeling such as being frustrated, defensive, resentful and worrying; and it's likely that these feelings were over things that, one week later, you'd consider 'small'.

The next day you were on a high, and not much would upset you.

If you can manage your 'self' to get more 'highs' you'll achieve far, far more of what you have chosen to achieve, and feel you are being more successful.

Run Your Mind Like a Car

Avoid Slipping Into a Negative Gear, Instead of Driving Forward in Positive

We can run our minds much as we drive a car. Indeed, man is the only animal who has the facility to make a choice about how to run his mind.

All other animals run on automatic.

When we have a low day, often the mind has slipped almost unnoticed into a negative gear – rather like slipping into reverse. The trouble is, we seldom notice it has happened.

What we need to do is to learn to get out of that negative gear, and decide to run our minds in a positive gear.

Recognize When You Slip Into Negative

Here are some typical 'vibes' that slip your mind into a negative gear.

You feel bad. You want to hit back at someone. You want to get even. You feel others are criticizing you unfairly. You feel in a rut. You feel depressed, unappreciated. You worry about things: mistakes in the past; something in the future. You feel fed up, lifeless. You feel tired, angry, annoyed.

You can also be physically tired; too tired to think clearly; too caught up in work; all work and no play; too much tension and stress; easily irritated.

You can wallow in some of these feelings. You rehearse in your mind, 'That's what I should have said'; 'I'll show them how wrong that is'; 'I'll get even'; 'I'll put her in her place'; 'I'm too tired right now'; 'There's no point in trying that idea'; 'Someone else will probably have done that already'.

The more you rehearse these things in your mind the worse you feel.

Continuing to Drive in Negative Gear

Have a Bad Day!

A man wakes up early – fifteen minutes too early. He regrets it, feeling he hasn't had quite enough sleep. He feels tired. He goes down to breakfast. His wife makes an unexpected request for him to remember something that day. He snaps. She snaps back. They argue. He leaves the house with a polite peck. He goes to buy his paper. His mind is elsewhere. The newspaper seller gruffly asks him what he wants. He feels annoyed at the seller's attitude.

He turns round and someone bumps into him without saying sorry. The train is a couple of minutes late. He gets a bit angry; spends the time rehearsing the scene with his wife. Sees the person on the platform who bumped into him and feels angry again. He looks the sort who wouldn't care about manners. On the train, he feels someone unfairly got the seat he should have had. By the time he gets to work it's already 'a bad day'. He gets upset at the first 'bad' sign. The people around him think that's unfair, and react back to him. He insists. By now he's feeling physically bad and has a bit of a headache. He doesn't handle things as diplomatically as he normally would. People react back. There are arguments. And so on.

By the end of the day, he is absolutely shattered, and in no state to repair the relationship at home. He comes in, wanting to do nothing but eat and slump in front of the TV because 'he's had a bad day'.

Familiar? How often have *you* had a day like that? Be honest . . .

What has happened is that one 'bad' experience has put him in a negative gear and he hasn't got out of it. This has made him take a negative view of all subsequent experiences. He can only think negatively, and everything is exaggerated. Others pick up the mood and react back. His negative perceptions keep him in negative gear, making everything about the day negative.

These are the ways our mind runs in negative gear. The problem is that it's a very easy gear of life to slip into. You don't have to think, just continue in a bad way. You have to learn to make a deliberate action to change out of it.

You need to take deliberate action because there will always be more opportunities to slip into negative gear than to get into positive:

- far more hours worrying about passing the exam than hours celebrating passing it. And once you've passed one exam you start worrying about the next.
- more things in the in-tray that upset you than please you.
- people give you more blank faces which you interpret as unfriendly than smiles which you interpret as friendly.
- it seems easier for the mind to interpret what someone says negatively rather than positively.

Continue like that, and you'll never be successful. You'll be in a low more often than on a high. You're just not managing your 'self' to achieve the things you've chosen to want.

Get Into Positive Gear

You can manage your mind every day, and every hour.

What you need to be able to do is to move it into positive gear at will.

The gear you seek to get into is the feeling of being on a high, on a roll, of everything going right, feeling good. In this state you are powerful and get things done.

The secret is to be able to switch out of negative into positive. You can do this. Simply. By managing your mind. And it just takes a few seconds to switch gears.

Firstly, realize that how you feel comes from what your thoughts are. 'Feeling down' is not something you catch from someone else, like 'flu. Similarly, the feeling of wanting to get even is not caused by what others have done. It is caused by *internal thoughts* – how we react internally to what happens in life.

Managing 'self' is managing our internal thoughts. Unfortunately, in today's life, our internal thoughts may automatically slip – unless we manage them. But many of these thoughts are untrue or just unreal imaginings. They are a misinterpretation of life. But these thoughts, even though unreal, do cause real feelings.

There are two problems to manage:

1 You choose the wrong frame of reference, and slip into negative.

You are angry because your spouse is late, yet again. You specifically asked him not to be late, because it is important that you get to the party on time. He just doesn't seem to care. It doesn't matter to him if he's late. You get angry. You rehearse what you'll say when he arrives. You'll make sure it doesn't happen again. Your internal thoughts drive your mood. You have a real, angry feeling.

Then the phone rings. It's the police. Your husband is in hospital seriously hurt. In a car crash. He was going too fast, to get to your appointment on time. For the sake of 5 minutes or so. How do you feel now?

It was the first *unreal*, thoughts that caused you to have the feeling of anger.

2 Your mind doesn't filter things out, and lets through all sorts of unreal thoughts, which slip you into negative gear.

What I want you to do now is to *not* think of a mob of angry people outside your house. The *last* thing I want you to think of is angry people outside your house.

But what have you just thought of? The subconscious mind lets it through.

Since your mind can trigger – mistakenly – the wrong frames of reference, and can let through unreal negative thoughts, why not decide to run your mind with the sort of thoughts and interpretations you want to have? Most people don't make many conscious choices. They simply let their minds wander. They wake up in a good mood or a bad mood. Good luck lifts them up. Bad luck drives them down. They are not driving their minds – they are simply reacting to random thoughts.

That's why it's true to say, 'you can be as happy as you make up your mind to be'.

Man is the only animal with the capacity to choose how he thinks. Every other animal thinks reactively. So why not use this extra power, rather than react like a hound when it sees a fox, or a sheep following another sheep.

Here are 25 one-minute exercises to stop you slipping into negative, and change to driving in positive.

Just one minute can change you from a low to a high. Just one minute can change your whole day. Whenever you feel yourself going low or slipping into negative, take 60 seconds out and try one of the 25 ideas that follow.

Exercise 1

Recognize that it is possible to see things in a different frame.

Look at this picture.

Figure 3

What do you see? An old lady or a young lady? Study it hard. Which? If you see a young lady can you also see an old lady? If you see an old lady can you also see a young lady?

Now look at Figure 4. Does that help? Look also at Figure 5. Does that help? Now realize the following:

Figure 4

Figure 5

- your mind sees things in different ways. Often the first way your mind interprets something isn't the only way, and it's often the wrong way.
- if you precondition people for one second by showing them Figure 4 first, they'll see a young lady in the picture. If they instead see Figure 5 for one second, they'll see an old lady in the same picture. Preconditioning massively affects your first thoughts and thus your feelings.

Choose to precondition your mind positively.

Take one minute to remember the old lady/young lady picture; and remember that how you feel is dictated by the frame of reference for incoming data. So decide in this minute to interpret all incoming data in the most positive and charitable way you can.

Exercise 2

Take one minute to let your mind have an internal *positive* dialogue to replace any accidental negative ones.

Often you allow your mind to talk to itself in a negative way: talking to yourself in a depressed way; talking to yourself about how bad others' actions are and how they upset you; talking to yourself about how bad others are towards you; talking to yourself about how bad life is.

Decide instead to make your mind talk to itself positively in this one minute:

'I'm absolutely unique in this world, there's no one else like me.'

'I'm doing well because I'm thinking about what I want to do, and doing it.'
'I'll make this week the best week of my life.'
'I can make someone else happy.'
'I can win, I can succeed.'
'I can be as happy as I decide to be.'
'Let me count my blessings, not my troubles.'

Exercise 3

Take one minute each morning and *start out* to make the day positive.

Early each morning make a 'Just for Today' list.

Just for today:

I will not try to change things I cannot change.
I will be active and energized all day.
I will be happy.
I will make others happy.
I will be as likeable as I can be.
Today, in every way, I'm going to get better and better.
Today is a new life to this wise man/woman.
Today is the first day of the rest of my life.
I'll enjoy today as though I'm on summer holiday.

In the minute you take, re-read these thoughts.

Exercise 4

Stop everything and *take one minute* for yourself. Sit and think. Choose your attitude. Change your attitude and change your day. Right now, take one minute to change your attitude for the rest of today.

Exercise 5

Take one minute to do one little thing to spoil yourself. For no-one else. For you. Go on. Do it. If you can't spoil yourself now, think for one minute how you can spoil yourself later.

Exercise 6

Take one minute to decide to clear today of past regrets and future fears. Stop dwelling on what might have been or what might happen.

This day will never come again in your life. Live it. Don't waste it by trying to relive yesterday or live tomorrow before it's due. What is the date today? Remember it for the rest of your life as the day you decided, from now on, to live each day to its fullest.

Exercise 7

Take one minute and deal with a worry. Decide to do three things to stop it.

1 Write down now the worst thing that can happen to you at the moment.
2 Reconcile yourself to this. Live it, imagine it, accept it.
3 Now work out ways you can improve on the worst.

Do you have a worry? Tackle it this way, now.

Exercise 8

Take one minute to decide how much bother and stress a worry is worth – and refuse to give it any more. Is it worth 10 minutes, 1 hour, 12 hours, 1 hour a day for a week, for a month? Exactly how much is it worth? Choose an amount. And give it no more.

Exercise 9

Take one minute to not let little things ruin your happiness. Why should they? Wait for something big if anything is going to ruin it. Why waste your happiness on little things?

Exercise 10

Take one minute to eliminate the effects of any unjust remark. Close your eyes. Remember the words said. Now make them fuzzy, and quieter and quieter. And more and more slurred . . .Try it now, this minute. Doesn't that put them into perspective?

Exercise 11

Take one minute to get rid of negative thoughts arising from a written remark. Close your eyes. Look at the words on the paper in your mind. Make them smaller and smaller. Right down to the size of a postage stamp. Then imagine yourself rising up and seeing them from the ceiling. How small they are and how inconsequential. Try it now, this minute.

Exercise 12

Take one minute to get rid of your internal dialogue and any debate within yourself. Close your eyes. Turn down its volume in your mind. Make it softer and softer and softer. More and more warbled. Finished. Try it this minute.

Exercise 13

Take one minute to get rid of your troubles. Sit in a chair. Picture yourself taking each trouble out of your mind and writing it down on a piece of paper. Pile up the paper troubles on the floor beside you. One by one. The pile gets bigger and bigger. Then set a match to it. Do it this minute.

Exercise 14

Take one minute to remember a pleasant experience. Close your eyes. In your mind make it louder; bigger; closer; more joyful; more colourful; warmer. Doesn't that feel good? Do it this minute.

Exercise 15

Take one minute to decide to act for one week exactly how you want to. Act as if you felt better, happier than you've ever been; act as though you're clearly going to succeed. Act now as though you're on a high, and you will soon be on one. Go on, decide to do it for the rest of the day from this minute.

Exercise 16

Take one minute to put a picture in your mind of how you *don't* want to be – grumpy, ill-tempered, defeated. Now replace it in a star-burst with a picture of what you do want to be. Try it this minute.

Exercise 17

Take one minute to take some exercise. Get active. Run up the stairs. Walk up and down the corridor. Go on, now, this minute.

Exercise 18

Take one minute to relax. Learn to do a one-minute relaxation. Breathe in slowly for 10 seconds, hold for 10 seconds, release for 10 seconds. Do it twice. Now. How do you feel? (OK – steal another minute and do it twice again).

Exercise 19

Help someone else take one minute out for *themselves*. Try to create a bit of happiness for someone else, now. Go on, do something nice for someone else. Call them. Now. How do you feel?

Exercise 20

Take one minute to decide never to waste a minute thinking about people you don't like. They aren't worth it.

Exercise 21

Take one minute to remember that the whole world isn't against you. There are billions of people who don't give a damn about you (one way or the other). So why let others upset your 'high'?

Exercise 22

Take one minute to decide not to expect thanks from anyone. That way you'll never be disappointed. People rarely say thank you. It's not anything to do with you. People just don't.

Exercise 23

Take one minute to decide not to expect the in-tray to be full of goodies. In any pile of things there will be 3 or 4 baddies. That's usual. Expect 5 in any pile. Identify them as they come. And feel great if it's under 5.

Exercise 24

Take one minute to decide not to allow anyone else to make you feel inferior. No one can make you feel this way unless *you* decide yourself to feel inferior. There is no need for you to feel that way, ever.

Exercise 25

Finally, take your last minute of the day to decide to not worry at all about what others may be saying or thinking about you. Most people aren't worrying about you – they are far too busy with themselves. How many people would take time off work to come to your funeral? Most people in this world who upset you would be far more concerned about something trivial in their own lives, like a cold, than by the news of your death. Aren't you silly to let even one day of your life or one hour of your life be ruined by anyone who would not even come to your funeral?

In one minute you can switch yourself from slipping into neutral (or reverse) to driving in top by any one of the above 25 ways. Try a minute on each and every one. Frequently. Then you'll really live great days.

Next Steps

Write a list in your pocket book to help remind you of the 25 ways to use a minute to switch from slipping negative to driving in positive:

1 Old lady/young lady
2 Positive internal dialogue
3 Make a 'Just for Today' list
4 Change your attitude, change your day
5 Spoil yourself
6 Stop worrying. Live for today
7 Take three steps to stop worrying
8 Decide how much anxiety it's worth
9 Don't let little things ruin your happiness
10 Scramble unjust remarks
11 Reduce bad written comments to their real, inconsequential size
12 Turn down the internal dialogue volume

13 Set fire to your troubles
14 Make pleasant things bigger
15 Act how you want to feel
16 Replace a bad picture with a good one
17 Get active
18 Relax
19 Help someone else
20 Ignore people you don't like
21 Billions couldn't care less
22 Don't expect thanks
23 Expect bad in-trays
24 Don't feel inferior
25 If they won't come to your funeral, don't let them upset you now

Now you know how to manage yourself, let's move on to how you can manage other people.

Day 6

Get Others To Do
What You Want

Other people are often major obstacles to happiness and success. Now you know your goals; you are planning what to do; you can manage your time; and you can manage your 'Self'. But other people really can greatly affect your life.

The methods for managing others are not new. They can be found in the Bible, the Koran, and all number of books and courses. Managing others doesn't really require much new wisdom. What you need is the determination to apply the methods you know will work.

The problem is that it is far easier to not bother – to relax and react to what other people say and do. It's easier to be negative or unpleasant with others than it is to be positive and pleasant.

It's also easier to argue than to negotiate; to complain rather than to understand; to shout rather than to listen. Easier to sulk than to sympathize. Easier to order than to explain. Easier to criticize than to compliment. Easier to demand rather than to ask.

You know, however, that you will need to use the age-old methods for working with and managing other people. Indeed your success may not be decided so much by how much you do, but by how much you can get other people to do for you and, more important, with you.

And you know you won't get them to do much by arguing, complaining, shouting, ordering, demanding and criticizing them.

There are just three basic skill areas to work on, and each has some age-old methods to apply, consistently.

- Motivating and influencing others
- Asking for what you want
- Negotiating and bargaining

We'll take them in turn.

Skill 1

Six age-old magic methods to motivate and influence people

There are just six age-old magic methods you need to know. They have come down to us through the ages. Most of us know these by experience, but we are generally too lazy actually to practise them. We think it's quicker to get people to do things by just telling them or persuading them by force of argument, or logic. This isn't the quickest or best way to get anyone to do something. If, however, you exercise all of the six magic methods regularly, you'll succeed easily. Even if you can do three out of six each day, you'll do very well, although most people tend to practise only one or two.

Whenever you are dealing with people – and that's most of the time – remember people are *people*. A simple mnemonic is:

The 6 magic methods to get people to do things:

a**P**preciate others
don't argu**E**
Offer to help
ap**P**reciate others more
Listen first
influenc**E** more than persuade

Appreciate Others

You give your nearest and dearest many things – support, guidance, care, protection, food, clothing, money. You give other people many other things – presents, Christmas cards, money as a tip for service.

But you rarely give even your loved ones the thing they crave most: your appreciation and praise of them. Indeed, your loved ones might even die without knowing how good you think they are. Don't leave it until death-bed time. Don't leave it until retirement speeches. Don't leave it until annual appraisal time. Don't leave it until the moment is 'right' (it rarely is). Do it now and do it regularly.

Give people credit, praise and appreciation.

If you find this difficult, choose one of the virtues below that may apply to them.

Let them know you value their alertness, adaptability, appreciativeness, attentiveness, candour, capability, caring, concern, conscientiousness, consideration, constructiveness, cooperation, creativity, daring, decisiveness, determination, efficiency, fairness, frankness, friendliness, good nature, humour, ingenuity, initiative, kindness, logic, meticulousness, openness, objectivity, practicality, professionalism, reliability, responsiveness, self confidence, tolerance, understanding, veracity or warmth.

Avoid criticism wherever you can. If you have to be critical and call attention to other people's mistakes try to do it indirectly, and compensate it with praise for something else.

Catch people doing something right – instead of spending your time catching them doing something wrong.

Agree, Don't Argue

The only sure way to win an argument is to avoid it.

If there is an argument, the only way you can move forward is to change your opponent, change the subject, or change yourself. Start with changing yourself. When you are wrong, admit it bravely and openly.

Never tell people they are wrong. Respect their opinions. Respect them. Let the other person save his or her face.

Talk about your mistakes first. Forgive and forget. Don't be afraid to lose in order to win – to give way on one point to win another.

Get the other person to say 'yes' to something. Get the other person nodding.

Don't use logic on a closed mind. Open it first.

Offer to Help

The only way to get what you want is to help others to get what they want. People are far more interested in themselves than they are in you. Position things in terms of the other person's interests, not only yours. Show the other person how he can get something he will like.

Remember that what people really want may be different from what they publicly say they want. Everybody wants credit, recognition, praise, increase in self-esteem, even though they never say they want these things. Offer to help them get these things.

Appreciate More

The single best way to motivate others is to show your appreciation of what they are, or what they've done. So, show your appreciation even more.

Listen

Listen to people first, before you ask them to listen to you. Do this actively, earnestly, even when you don't want to, or feel it's a waste of time.

Where there is stress, tension, niggling, conflict or irritation, resolve it by listening, and empathize with what others are feeling and saying. See things from their point of view.

Once you have listened and think you've understood, listen one more time.

Always try to understand the other person thoroughly before trying to make yourself understood.

Influence, Rather Than Persuade

Ask a question instead of ordering directly.

Let the other person feel the idea is his. Make the other person feel good about doing what you suggest. Never leave the other person feeling beaten.

These are just six methods to work on to get others to help you get what you want out of life. They make up the word PEOPLE. We all know they work. They are easy to do. In fact, they are so easy that we most often decide not to bother with them. We decide it's easier or quicker to criticize, argue, persuade or talk them into it. But then we motivate nobody.

Ching-Li-Fa

The Chinese believe the order of priority of ways to get people to do things is Ching-Li-Fa.

First they try Ching. If that really fails they go to Li. And at the end of their tether they go to Fa.

Ching is the relationship between people: 'I will do this for you because I know you, like you, trust you or your family'. If this doesn't work the Chinese will resort to Li, Logic: 'This is why it makes sense to do it'. And as an absolute final resort they'll go to Fa, the law or the contract: 'The agreement says we should do it'.

The Chinese notice, however, that Westerners use the opposite order, Fa-Li-Ching. The first reason to get someone to do something is because it's the law, or in the agreement or the contract: 'You must do it'. If this fails, the Westerners resorts to logic: 'It makes sense anyway'. As an absolute last resort, the Westerner will use the idea of 'Well, let's have a drink together, and see if you can't just do this for me'.

Thus the Westerner, visiting China and with only eight hours available, will say:

'Let's get down to business, then have dinner together if we have time.'

The Chinese will say:

'Let's have dinner first, then get down to business if we have time.'

Using the order Ching-Li-Fa, like the Chinese, will bring you many dividends.

Skill 2

Ask For What You Want

The easiest way to get something is to ask for it, nicely. Yet this is one of our most under-used tools. Most people go forever without asking for what they want. We have an in-built fear of being rebuffed, of being made to look foolish, or we're quite simply too proud. We feel embarrassed to ask. But 'Don't ask, don't get' is more than an aphorism.

Since most of us don't ask often enough, our Asking Muscle grows weak. It is a good thing to build that muscle. Like any other, the more you exercise it the stronger it will get. The stronger your Asking Muscle gets, the more successful you will be.

Here's how to develop your Asking Muscle:

1 Work out what it is that you need. Ask for exactly that.
2 Don't feel embarrassed about asking. Do it. Once you've done it, it's easier to do it again.
3 Realize that people can feel flattered and pleased to be asked. Show that you appreciate and respect them for their opinion.

4 Ask a person, not a company or an organisation.

5 Ask for help. Don't beg.

6 Give people a reason why they should want to say yes.

7 Ask, and keep asking, using different approaches. Don't worry about rejection. In the end, the more you ask for, the more you'll get. Get used to asking.

Skill 3

Bargain and Negotiate For What You Want

Most people dislike bargaining. They feel that the other party will outsmart them or take advantage of them. So they don't bargain.

Most people also have a fear of negotiating. It seems a complicated subject. We hear regularly of 'trade union negotiations' that seem to be so complicated they go on for days or weeks. Heavy books are written on how to negotiate. But that needn't be a turn-off.

The reality is that we bargain and negotiate all the time. Children are great at it. They negotiate:

to stay out late (and even how late . . .)
for more pocket money
for how long their hair can be
to wear the clothes they want
how early they can wear make-up
to stay the night at a friend's house.

Their secret is that they know exactly what they want and are determined to push for it.

You, too, can decide to bargain or negotiate to get:

the salary you want for a new job
your children into a particular school
the plumber to come, today
the bank charges waived
a house for less
the landlord to repair the roof this week
more time for something you really want to do.

The Simple Man's Guide

Your Weapons

Whether you bargain or negotiate there are only three things to think about to help you succeed in getting what you want. Prepare fully by increasing the firepower of these three weapons.

Weapon 1

Your Information

If an issue is going to be price, what are the prices of similar objects in other places? Are they selling fast at these prices? What price have you bought one at before? What price does the seller really need or want? How can the price vary if you pay cash, today? What are the advantages to the seller of making a sale quickly? What position is the seller in? What pressure is on him?

You can obtain much of your most helpful information before you start talking. But an equal amount can come from the early part of your discussions by asking questions and listening to the other party.

Weapon 2

Your Power

Spend time identifying the power you have. It is always more than you think it is. For example, identify:

your freedom to go to a competitor
the power of any precedent already set – he has done something similar before
having other options – you don't have to do this
your nuisance value – you can be very awkward
the power of hierarchy – you can go to the 'boss'

Weapon 3

Your Time

Get time on your side:

start negotiations before the other person realizes what
you are doing
remove the barriers to being in a hurry
prepare, and know, a private 'best acceptable' option if
you fail to get total agreement
prepare a list for the other party of the advantages of
agreeing under time pressure

You can dramatically improve the power of each of your
weapons by thinking about them fully beforehand.

Weapon 4

Your Strategy

Once you've worked on your weapons increasing your
information, recognizing the knowledge of the power you
have, and getting time on your side, then decide the
strategy. There are two broad approaches:

Strategy 1: Bargain

This is a win-lose approach. The cake is divided. Whatever
you gain the other person loses and vice-versa. Many price
discussions are like this.

Strategy 2: Negotiate

This is a win-win approach. You may make the cake bigger; or consider different cakes, with different decorations. Add in some bread and jam. You both win – he likes the icing and you don't; he doesn't like the cream and you do.

All-Time Truths About Hard Bargaining

Bargaining is most frequently used in 'one-off' deals.

When you bargain, the following very simple tactics can help you, in most situations, to get what you want:

- Take a very extreme initial position. Start very high indeed, even if the justification for this is only superficial. But the justification needs to be sufficiently reasonable to not be dismissed out-of-hand.
- Lower the other person's expectations. It's good if you can start to do this even before the other party realizes you are starting to bargain.
- Avoid concessions, e.g. by making your authority limited: 'I can't agree to that on my own', 'I'll have to ask the rest of the family'.
- Use emotional tactics. Shout, get angry; if needed go red in the face. This tactic is particularly useful in public places – restaurants, queues at airline desks, etc, where embarrassment can get you a quick, favourable, face-saving response.

But remember, such tactics are unlikely to make you many friends or cause the person to want to bargain with you again.

All-Time Truths About Good Negotiating

Most of the time when you are trying to succeed by getting others to do what you want, you are dealing with people who you will need to work with again and again. They may be family, colleagues or acquaintances. You will be better off trying to find a solution where you will both win – that way you'll get even more help in the future. You need, therefore, to negotiate rather than to bargain.

Decide beforehand your best acceptable option to a negotiated agreement – and be prepared to walk away if you don't get it . . .

- Decide to be hard on the problem, soft on the person.
- Build trust with the other person. Listen with empathy. Try to really understand all his or her needs.
- Work out the whole range of what could be of value to the other party. Consider all the soft benefits (such as better self-esteem, better reputation) as well as the hard benefits (such as money).
- Focus on understanding the underlying interests that cause a certain 'position' to be taken.
- Explore all the ways to achieve mutual benefit, including inventing ways together.
- In trying to achieve your own, private, best acceptable option, suggest that both of you look at the problems from the point of view of a hypothetical third party expert – what, for instance, would a judge or an accountant say if they looked at this situation.

These very simple hints will help you to get what you want – and so be successful – when managing others. They cover motivating and influencing others to help get what you want, asking for what you want, and learning to bargain and negotiate for what you want. The hints are very simple, but time after time they are not followed. If you manage to follow them for even one day a week you will become more successful than most other people at getting what you want.

Next Steps

1 Write in your pocket notebook and in your diary the six key ways to motivate PEOPLE.

a**P**preciate others
don't argu**E**
Offer to help
ap**P**reciate others more
Listen
influenc**E** more than persuade

Plan that at the end of each day you'll examine whether you are using all six truths. Concentrate on a different one for each day of the week. Build up from using two each day to three, four, five, then six.

2 Write 'Ching-Li-Fa' in your pocket notebook.

3 Write 'Ask' in your pocket notebook. Plan to check at the end of each day how many things you've asked for that day, beyond routine work issues. Plan to develop your Asking Muscle.

4 Write in your pocket notebook: 'Decide to bargain or negotiate'. To do these well, 'prepare in advance how to use information, power and time'.

5 Write down the all-time truths about bargaining; and the all-time truths about negotiating.

On the last day we'll talk about the most exciting part of the whole One Week Way – putting it into practice . . .

Day 7

Do Something Next

You have now reached the end of this book. It has outlined a very simple way to achieve personal success: six day-by-day steps to help you to choose what you want and then achieve it. As I said at the beginning, it's easy when you know how.

But Day 7 is the most important step – deciding what to do next.

Here is how you should think about what to do next, and how you should feel as you start afresh on a completely new way of being successful in life.

1 What To Do

- Remember that, without this final step, you haven't really started. So buy yourself that pocket notebook and pocket diary.
- Perhaps begin by writing in the key points at the end of each chapter.
- 'Where' you begin isn't half as important as 'when'. And the answer to that is 'now'. It doesn't matter what you do as long as you do something. If you don't fancy starting at page 1, then start somewhere else – maybe

with something that strikes a chord. You may feel that exercising your Asking Muscle is the first step you need to take. Do it. Or maybe you would prefer to start with managing your self. Begin there. But do it now!

- Remember you don't have to do it all immediately. Working on any one of the exercises will help you towards success. And working on it for even one hour a week is much, much better than not doing any of it at all.

   That's why simply making a start – *now* – is so important.

- You can start slowly . . .but build up. Clearly, the more of the book you do apply, and the more frequently you apply it, the more successful you are likely to be.

- Remember, most of us can't apply all of these ideas, all of the time. But the closer you get, the better things will be. So learn to enjoy the feeling of dipping into the book again and again to remind yourself of exercises, and of getting better and better at doing more and more of them, more and more of the time.

2 How to Feel

Feel good. No, feel great! You should feel like this because:

- You know the 'secret way the magic trick is done', which very few other people know.
- You know it's easy because you know how, whereas others will struggle.
- You know you are unique. There is no one else on earth at all like you.
- From reading this book you already have some good ideas of what you want out of life.

- You already have some ideas that will work for you on how to manage your life-time and get things done; on how to avoid the routine and do what's important to you.
- You know how to manage your 'self'; how to stop yourself feeling down and negative; and how to switch yourself into positive gear. What a marvellous gift. You can feel 'up' instead of 'down'.
- You have some good ideas about what you can try to get others to do what you want; how to influence others; how to negotiate or bargain; and how to ask for what you want.

Most of all, you have developed some great ideas on how to make next year the best year of your life, next month the best month, next week the best week. Decide to make today the best day. Because today is the start of the rest of your life. And today you can decide to try the *One Week Way to Personal Success*. Do it, it will work for you, and enjoy the rest of your life.

Appendix

Complete This Only at the End of Month 1

	Almost Never	Seldom	Often	Almost Always
1 I carry a personal pocket notebook				
2 I carry a personal pocket diary				
3 I have my funeral oration written, and periodically revise it				
4 I have written my 'lightning will strike' plan, and periodically revise it				
5 I have written a life pattern, and regularly rewrite it				
6 I regularly write a 'wish/want and dream' list				
7 I regularly write a list of pick-me-ups and put-me-downs				
8 I have a list of lifetime goals, and regularly review it				

	Almost Never	Seldom	Often	Almost Always
9 I have a list of what I want to achieve in the next six months, and regularly review it				
10 I know the things that make today a better day, next week a better week				
11 I list my goals in 'A', 'B', 'C' sequence				
12 I plan my activities in 'A', 'B', 'C' sequence				
13 I spend most of my time and effort on 'A' goals and 'A' activities				
14 I spend more and more of my time on the top floor of life ('important but not urgent')				
15 I spend less and less of my time in the basement ('neither important nor urgent')				
16 I regularly ask myself 'What's the best use of these moments, now?'				
17 I plan each week				
18 I start each day with a 'To Do' list				
19 I use an LBW drawer				
20 I deliberately plan a 'Not to do' list				
21 I say 'No' regularly				
22 I set aside peak periods for important things				
23 I don't put off unpleasant things				
24 I read my 25 exercises to get positive				

	Almost Never	Seldom	Often	Almost Always
25 I feel I can get out of neutral into top gear				
26 Each day I do 10 out of the 25 one-minute exercises				
27 I read the magic methods on people				
28 I consciously use three out of the six people methods each day				
29 I try to use Ching before I invoke Fa				
30 Each day I stretch my Asking Muscle				
31 I prepare for bargaining by understanding information, power and time				
32 I prepare my tactics for bargaining or negotiating				
33 I follow the age-old methods to bargain				
34 I follow the age-old methods to negotiate				
35 I feel I am doing more and more of the above things more often				
36 I reread the *One Week Way to Personal Success*				
37 I now feel more successful				
38 I feel the next year can be my best year				
39 I feel the next month can be my best month				
40 I feel I know how to make tomorrow the best day of my life				

Award yourself 1 point for Almost Never, through to 4 points for Almost Always. Check your score next month and then a month later. If you are becoming successful, your score will be going up, getting over 100 and on towards 160. Eventually your score will be so high, you will feel so good about it, that you will want to pass on the *One Week Way to Personal Success* to someone else.

Books That Have Helped

Six of the Best

Carnegie, Dale, *How to Enjoy Your Life and Your Job*, Cedar Books.

Fanning, Tony and Robbie, *Get It All Done and Still Be Human*, Ballantine Books, New York.

Fisher and Ury, *Getting to Yes*, Business Books Ltd.

Lakein, Alan, *How to Get Control of Your Time and Your Life*, David McKay Co Ltd.

Le Bouef, Michael, *Working Smart*, Warner Books Inc.

Robbins, Anthony, *Unlimited Power*, Ballantine Books, New York.

Notes